AF375428

HAPPY 41ST BIRTHDAY, BRIAN: A TOAST TO HEALTH AND HAPPINESS!

Happy 41st Birthday, Brian: A Toast to Health and Happiness!

Carllos Nogueira

Getting to Know Brian

Brian Watts is my boyfriend, and in the two months that we've been together, I've discovered so many beautiful things about him. I want to spend more time getting to know him and also congratulate him on his 41st birthday. I want to highlight his strengths, skills, and achievements, celebrate this special day, and express my wishes for his dreams to come true, for good health, prosperity, and abundance. I am grateful for his life and for who he is.

Family is important to Brian, and he shares a loving relationship with family members and dear friends. He also cares for his 10-year-old dog named Adora. Brian is a vegetarian who prioritizes a healthy lifestyle, exercises at home, and radiates positive energy.

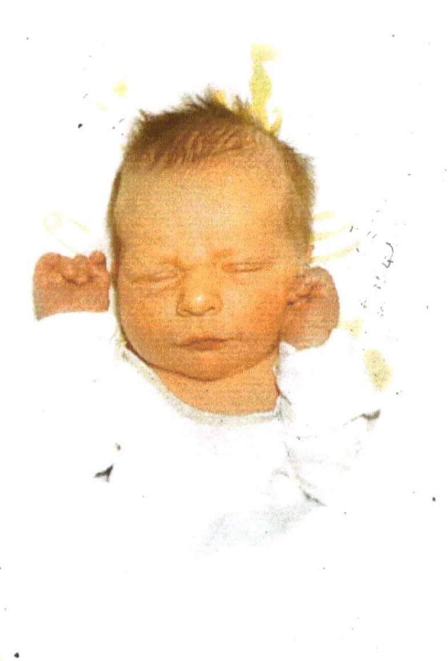

Brian was born in Middletown on December 11, 1982. He is a dedicated and responsible accountant, having studied and graduated in the field. Brian possesses a calm and seductive masculinity. He enjoys traveling and values organization. His home is a beautiful, cozy, and welcoming space. Traveling the world is one of his passions, with Thailand being his favorite destination. Brian has two protection tattoos, given by a Buddhist monk in Thailand.

Special Qualities

Affectionate Nature

His affectionate nature is evident in his warm hugs and the joy of touching him. I adore his blue eyes and his beautiful skin.

Shared Interests

We enjoy watching movies and series together, engaging in conversations, and sharing stories and experiences. Brian is an excellent advisor.

Patience and Calmness

He is patient when giving me driving instructions, polite, and exudes a calming presence.

I usually say he's like fabric softener, hahaha, with a pleasant scent that leaves everything soft.

As seen in this picture, his angelic, seductive, and captivating expression.

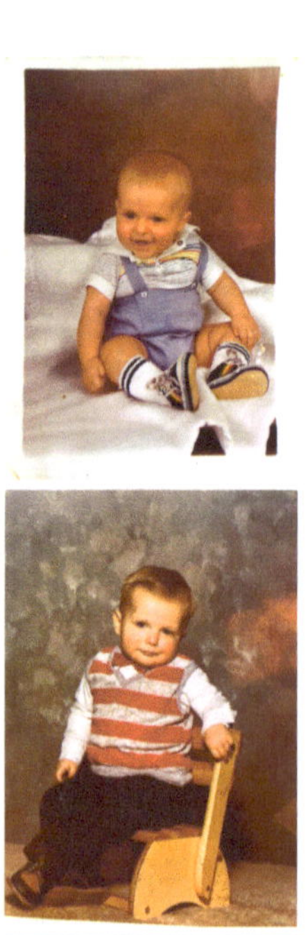

Childhood Memories

I came across some adorable childhood photos of Brian. He was truly a beautiful child.

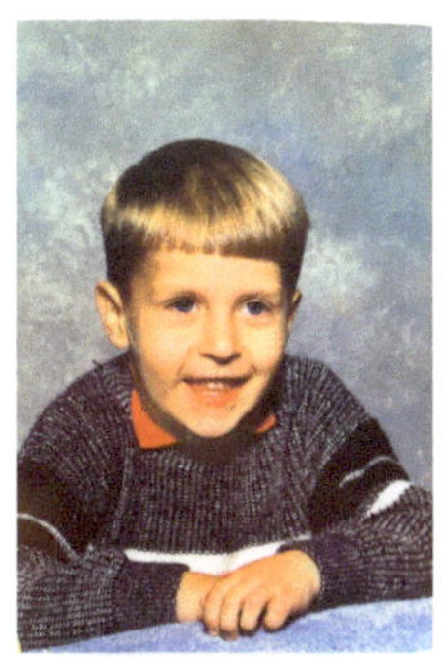

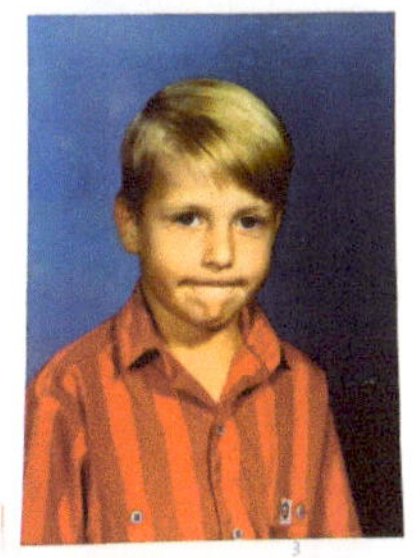

Brian Watts:
A Celebration of Love and Life

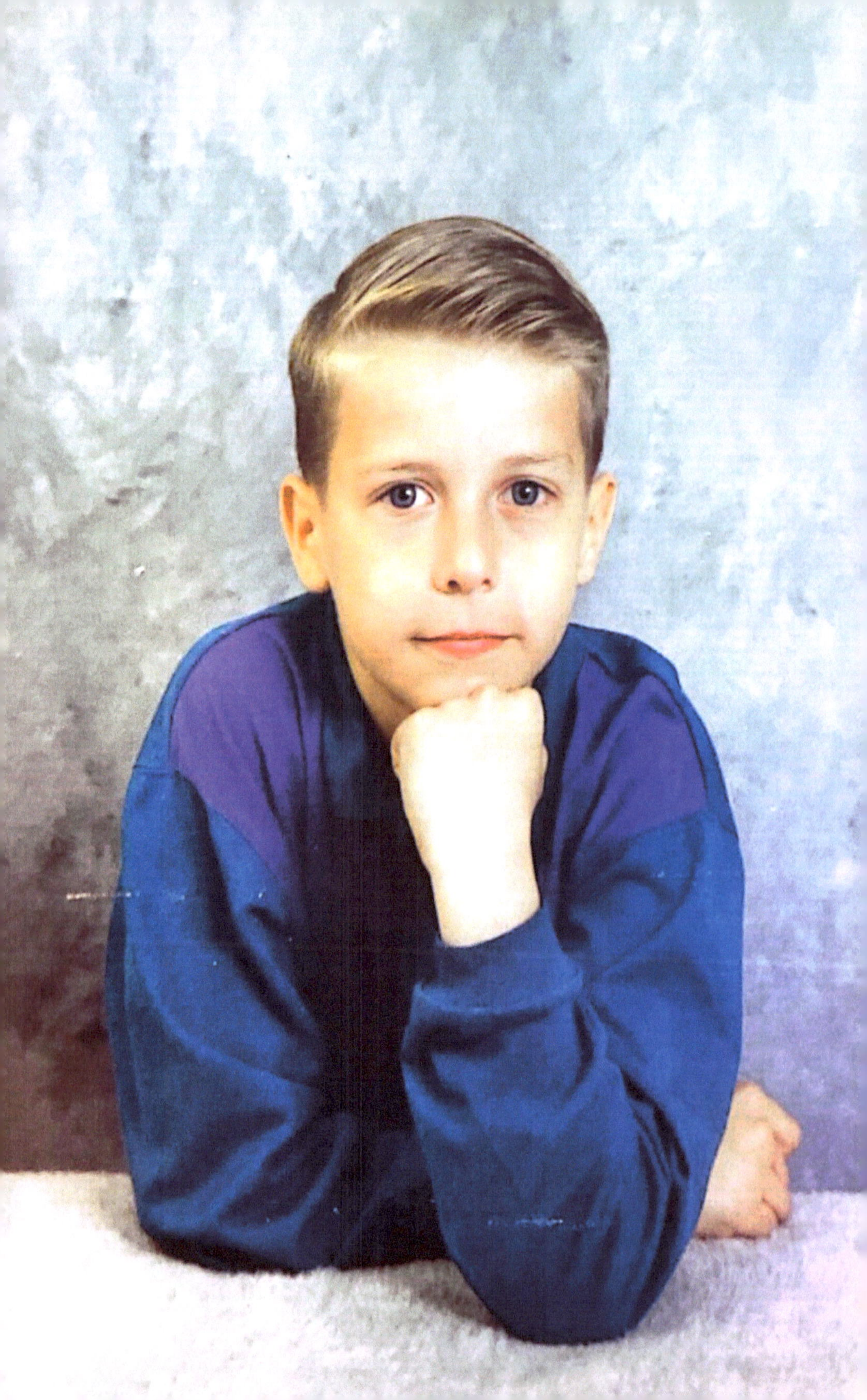

A Trip to Niagara Falls

MEMORABLE JOURNEY

Brian treated me to a wonderful trip to Niagara Falls. He drove for five hours each way, and the time we spent together in the car and at the falls was truly magical. The illuminated falls at night and the close encounter on a boat ride were spectacular. Feeling the water bless us as it splashed upon us was incredibly special. We have beautiful photos from this trip and enjoyed delightful meals at a restaurant for dinner and lunch.

ENCHANTING LOCATIONS

On our way back, we stopped at Watkins Glen and took a lovely walk in a picturesque location. We had a vegan meal in a charming roadside town. Finally, we dined at a Mexican restaurant upon our return, which was a beautiful ending to our journey.

Every new year is a blank page.
May you write a story filled with love and success.

HAPPY BIRTHDAY!

CELEBRATING ANOTHER YEAR
OF LIFE AND GRATITUDE.
MAY THIS UPCOMING YEAR BE
EVEN MORE AMAZING!

Shared Moments

Serenity on the Zephyr

The Zephyr float provided a serene and meditative moment of relaxation.

Meditation and Togetherness

Brian is both a conqueror and a companion. I loved when he joined me at the Buddhist center, meditating and sharing moments with the group.

Everyday Adventures

Brian is kind and chivalrous. We cook, shop, organize the home, do laundry, exercise, and meditate together. Even when we got lost in the Shawangunk Ridge Forest, I felt at ease knowing we would find our way together, which we did.

Trip to Guatemala Our first international journey and being part of the organization and this adventure has been incredible. Besides being a celebratory trip for the beautiful event of Brian's birthday, it's also a year-end closing and the beginning of a new cycle. Visiting Central America, observing, and exploring a volcano is undoubtedly something very beautiful.

Halloween Fun

Our Halloween in New York was a blast.

WE LOOKED FABULOUS IN WIGS,
AND THE COSTUMES WERE FUN.

Moments Together

First Date

Our initial conversation happened on Sunday, October 1, via Grindr. We officially met on October 4, 2023, in Bear Cliff, and I've kept the photo from that day close to my heart, alongside a beautiful sunset and a star-filled night.

Magical Snowy Day

Our snowy day together was magical. Playing with snowballs and then warming up with his comforting embrace was truly special.

Learning Italian and English Together

I admire Brian's determination to study Italian and his motivation and consistency. I appreciate his patience in helping me learn English, teaching me. Babbel is great, but our conversations are amazing.

Thanksgiving Celebration

Thanksgiving with his family was a heartwarming experience. We celebrated and indulged in delicious food. I loved getting to know his family.

Adora

Zodiac sign

The person born on December 11, 1982, has the zodiac sign of *Sagittarius* in Western astrology. Exploring some positive traits associated with the Sagittarius sign, I found:

Adventurous and Curious: Sagittarius typically have an adventurous nature and are always seeking new experiences and knowledge.

Optimism: They are known for their optimistic nature, seeing the positive side of life even in challenging situations.

Witty and Energetic: They possess a keen sense of humor and are often energetic and enthusiastic.

Generosity: They tend to be generous and willing to share what they have with others.

Independence: They value their freedom and independence, always seeking to expand their horizons.

Regarding the Chinese zodiac, the birthdate of December 11, 1982, is associated with the Year of the *Dog*, according to the Chinese horoscope. Positive traits associated with the Dog include **loyalty, honesty, and a protective** nature towards those they love.

And from what I've been getting to know about Brian, I can agree with what I've read.

I Wish You Life, long life
I wish you the luck of everything that is good
    Of all happiness, have the company
    Coloring the road in its most beautiful tone
    I wish you the rain on the balcony
    Watering the rosebush to bloom
    And sunny days to make your plans
In the simplest things there are to imagine
    I wish you the peace of a swallow
    In perfect flight, contemplating the sea
    And may the faith that moves any mountain
    Renew you always, make you dream
But if melancholy hours come
    That the sweet moon will come to stroke you.
And may the sweetest star be your guide
    Like a simple mother guiding you
    I wish you more than a thousand friends
    The poetry that every poet has waited for
    Heart of a child full of hope
    I Wish You Life, long life
    Wish You Life
    I Wish You Life, long life
I wish you the luck of everything that is good

Excerpt from the poem "Te desejo vida" by Flavia Wenceslau

Brian,

On this special day, I want to wish you the very best as you embrace a new cycle of life. May this year bring you joy, success, and countless memorable moments.

Happy Birthday!

I feel incredibly fortunate to be a part of your life, sharing in the celebration of this important date. Your presence adds so much love and happiness to my days.

As you blow out the candles and make your wishes, know that my biggest wish is for your continued happiness, health, and success in the coming year. Your journey is a beautiful adventure, and I am grateful to be walking it with you.

I love you. Here's to another year of shared laughter, love, and wonderful moments.

Cheers to you and your special day!

With all my love,
Carllos Nogueira